WOODPECKERS

WOODPECKERS

MARY ANN McDONALD

THE CHILD'S WORLD®, INC.

Photo Credits
Joe McDonald: front cover, 2, 6, 9, 10, 13, 15, 19, 20, 24,
26, 29, 30
Derrick Hamrick: 16, 23

Printed in the United States of America.

Library of Congress Cataloging-in-Publication Data
McDonald, Mary Ann
Woodpeckers/Mary Ann McDonald
p.   cm.
Includes index.
Summary: Describes the physical characteristics,
behavior, and life cycle of woodpeckers.
ISBN 1-56766-218-8
1. Woodpeckers--Juvenile literature.   [1. Woodpeckers.]
I. Title.
QL696.P56M42   1996
598.7'2--dc20   95-46109
                        CIP
                        AC

TABLE OF CONTENTS

You are alone in the woods. RAT - A - TAT - A - TAT! What was that noise you heard? There it is again. RAT - A - TAT - A - TAT! A flash of red, black, and white flies away from the tree. Now you know what made the knocking! A woodpecker was rapping on the tree.

Woodpeckers use their sharp beaks to peck holes into wood. They make these holes to look for food and to build nests. Sometimes, woodpeckers peck holes in telephone poles or in the sides of buildings. They have even pecked holes in the space shuttle while it was waiting to take off!

A male *hairy woodpecker* uses his beak to peck a hole in a tree.

WHERE DO WOODPECKERS LIVE?

There are over 180 kinds, or **species**, of woodpeckers in the world. They live in many places, from low forests to high mountains. They live in the cold lands of the far north and in the tropical jungle. In North America, there are twenty-two species of woodpeckers. Some areas, though, don't have any woodpeckers. There are no woodpeckers in Australia, Antarctica, or the Sahara Desert in Africa.

The *acorn woodpecker* is the only woodpecker species with a white eye.

Woodpeckers range in size from 7 inches up to almost 17 inches. The *downy woodpecker* is the smallest and the *pileated*(PIE-lee-ay-ted) *woodpecker* is the largest. All woodpeckers have very sharp and strong claws. This helps the woodpecker climb up and down tree trunks.

The pileated woodpecker is the largest woodpecker species.

WHAT IS DRUMMING?

Sometimes, woodpeckers peck loudly just to make noise. This is called **drumming**. Woodpeckers drum in late winter and early spring to attract a mate. The noise also tells other woodpeckers to stay away from their chosen area, or **territory**. Both male and female woodpeckers drum, but on different trees.

A woodpecker drums loudly to protect its territory.

WHERE DO WOODPECKERS NEST?

In the spring, each pair of woodpeckers looks for just the right tree. Once they find it, they peck a large hole for a nest. Woodpeckers use both live and dead trees for nesting. Most woodpeckers drill a new hole every year. Some of them use the same tree for several years. These trees soon look like Swiss cheese!

A woodpecker makes its nest in a hole in a tree.

Woodpeckers make simple nests. They don't line them with sticks or grass the way some birds do. Sometimes, they line the bottom of the nest with wood chips. Each kind of woodpecker makes a different-sized hole for entering the nest. The big pileated woodpecker makes an entrance hole four inches across. The little downy woodpecker makes an entrance hole only an inch and one-half across.

Pine sap circles the nest hole of a *red-cockaded woodpecker.*

Gila (HEE-luh) *woodpeckers* live in the deserts of the southwestern United States. There are no large trees in the desert. Instead, the gila woodpecker builds its nest in a large cactus. The prickly cactus spines help protect the baby woodpeckers from enemies.

Gila woodpeckers live in desert areas.

HOW ARE BABY WOODPECKERS BORN?

Most female woodpeckers lay between two and twelve eggs. One species, called the *flicker*, can lay up to seventeen eggs! Woodpecker eggs are snowy white. The male and female take turns sitting on the eggs to keep them warm, or **incubate** them. The eggs hatch in two weeks.

Woodpecker babies have no feathers at all when they hatch! The new feathers grow quickly. At first, the baby woodpeckers look as if they have spiked hair. But the feathers keep growing and getting fluffier. As soon as the young birds have all their feathers, they leave the nest. The young birds can fly almost as well as their parents.

Young woodpeckers grow their feathers while living in the nest.

The woodpecker parents keep the nest very clean. Baby woodpeckers leave their wastes in ready-made natural diapers. These diapers are white sacs and feel like soft leather. The adult woodpeckers pick up each sac with their beaks. They fly away from the nest before dropping the sac. This keeps bugs away from the baby woodpeckers.

An adult woodpecker keeps the nest clean.

Woodpeckers eat insects, spiders, caterpillars, fruit, and seeds. Ants are a favorite food of many woodpeckers. Woodpeckers also love to eat animal fat, or **suet**. You can attract woodpeckers to your backyard with suet. Just hang a wire box filled with beef suet from a tree. Downy, hairy, and *red-bellied woodpeckers* love to visit suet feeders.

Sapsuckers use their beaks to find insects.

Woodpeckers use their beaks to look for bugs. Their beaks are very strong. The can peck off large pieces of hard wood. Woodpeckers also have a very long tongue. The tongue has a small hook on its end. The hook helps to pull insects out of their hiding places. The tongue is also sticky, which helps it hold food.

Woodpeckers use their long tongues to search for ants.

ARE WOODPECKERS IN DANGER?

Woodpeckers have few enemies. Other birds, such as *wrens* and *starlings*, often steal their nest holes. Squirrels also fight them for these comfortable homes. Rattlesnakes sometimes climb trees to eat the eggs and the young.

Woodpeckers face a bigger danger, though. People keep building houses and cutting down forests. Many of the places where woodpeckers live are being destroyed. The *ivory-billed woodpecker* has already become **extinct**. Other species are in danger of dying out.

Squirrels often try to steal woodpecker nests.

Woodpeckers are an important part of our natural world. They eat lots of bugs that are real nuisances. They are also pretty to look at and fun to watch! People are helping these beautiful birds by working to save the forests in which they live.

An acorn woodpecker is beautiful and fun to watch.

GLOSSARY

drumming (DRUM-ing)
Pounding to make noise. A woodpecker drums on a tree to attract a mate and announce its territory.

extinct (ex-TINCKT)
No longer living. An animal that has died out— like dinosaurs.

incubate (INK-yoo-bate)
Keep warm. Woodpecker parents sit on their eggs to keep them warm until they hatch.

species (SPEE-sheez)
A separate kind of an animal. There are many different kinds, or species, of woodpeckers.

suet (SU-it)
Animal fat. Woodpeckers love to eat suet.

territory (TEAR-i-tore-e)
An area that an animal protects as its own. Woodpeckers defend their territories to keep out other woodpeckers.

INDEX